AF469748

Lady Cycling

What to Wear &
How to Ride

MISS F.J. ERSKINE

THE BRITISH LIBRARY

First published in 1897 by Walter Scott Ltd

This edition published in 2014 by

The British Library
96 Euston Road
London NW1 2DB

British Library Cataloguing in Publication Data
A catalogue record for this publication is available from
The British Library

ISBN 978 0 7123 5727 2

Designed and typeset in Caslon by illuminati, Grosmont
Printed in Hong Kong by Great Wall Printing Co. Ltd

Contents

I

Cycling: Its Health and Social Aspects

THE OTHER DAY I came across an exhaustive paper on whether, from an hygienic point of view, ladies should cycle. "Whether they should or not, ladies *are* cycling," the author said, "and so far the results seem to be extremely beneficial." On no point, however, has a hotter controversy raged. Perhaps, like other things, the awful tales one heard had a certain very small kernel of truth wrapped up in a great deal of exaggeration. As a matter of fact, the question as to whether it is good or bad for women to ride simply lies in a nutshell. If they ride fifty miles where ten ought to be their limit—in short, if in cycling they cast reason and common-sense to the four winds of heaven—*then*, beyond all doubt, cycling is harmful.

For example: women ought not to race, if they have the slightest regard for their own health; and if they do, it is a suicidal policy, which is bound to end in disaster—I say nothing of its influence on the sport. Cycling now is so firmly rooted amongst the sane members of the community, as an easy and cheap form of locomotion, that the racing woman will only hurt herself by her action.

As a healthful form of exercise, in moderation, cycling stands in an exceptionally favourable position. The initial cost of a machine is certainly almost as high as that of a pony—but, then, the pony requires its own *entourage*, to say nothing of a large amount of thought to keep it in good working order. Then to a pony must be added a cart—another £25, harness £7, shoeing, feeding, clothing, and a groom; whereas the cycle does not require more than a careful fifteen minutes' cleaning, and fair handling. Added to this, cycling is ceasing to be merely a fashionable recreation, and taking the more sober and useful *rôle* as a means to an end. And in this lies its strength. If cycling existed only because it was a fashion, its death-knell would have been struck long ago. But it is no mere butterfly sport. Cycling, pure and simple—the "wheels goin' wound," dearly loved of the once famous Budge and Toddie—is, when the acrobatic stage is over, very poor work. There is a well-defined limit to the antics one can play on bicycle-back. But a cycle is the key to so much enjoyment that we adopt the key because it opens out England and the Continent to us. We cyclers can prowl all over England, Scotland, Ireland, and Wales, by aid of these rubber-tyred hoops. By their help sketchers can sketch more than ever they could do before its advent, when a complicated study of local trains had to be made to get to the place and back. Archaeologists can pursue their hobbies with renewed zest—the cycle photographer is a ubiquitous figure all over our roads, which are fortunately benefiting largely by the fact that those responsible for their care are now cyclists themselves, and as a "fellow-feeling makes us wondrous kind" to ourselves, so holes and ruts, moraine-like tracks, and other causes of woe, are in a fair way of becoming matters of history—thanks to the cycle.

If a cycle is of untold use to those who live in the country, much more so is it to those who live in towns. Few, who have not experienced it, know the horrors of a hot, airless August night in London, when there is a dusky sky overhead,—hot walls, hot footpaths, hot odoriferous wood paving, and no escape. The underground is hot and stuffy, the omnibuses crowded, stifling, and jolty. Workers all day, who pine for fresh air, have a kind of dusty amalgam to breathe instead, and a tramp over the pavement only increases the nervous headache the sufferer feels a little air would cure.

The cycle has come to the rescue here. For years it has been doing a great deal of good to young men, who were off and away into the country as soon as ever business was done. Since then we have marched with the times, and women are doing their part in the various businesses to which they are admitted, and, as a natural sequence, they require change and relaxation as much as their male relatives. Then came the cycle-mania in France. That vivacious country has always taken kindly to the cycle, and, as most fashions come from Paris, it did not take long for the humdrum English cycling to blaze out into a fashion over here. But being by nature a nation of shop-keepers—*mercer folk*, our continental cousins amiably call us—whilst cycling became the fashion, it is even now less the *mode* than the utilitarian hobby. Ladies do their shopping on wheels; the Princesses are said to prefer their wheels to horses, "because they are handier;" country dwellers pay visits to their neighbours on two wheels—themselves the motive power—instead of employing the horse.

Many and many a lady does up her evening and night gear in a neat little bundle or a basket, and cycles off to spend a day or two with a friend who lives twenty or thirty miles off. People go out to dinner—on bicycles. They pay surprise visits by moonlight—on bicycles. They ride to the meet—on bicycles; and, what is more, many go across country in a fashion—on bicycles. Clergymen find the machine indispensable in working large, scattered country parishes. Teachers, tradesmen, high and low, rich and poor, see in the cycle a cheap and handy means of locomotion, and as such it will remain with us, not as a fashion, but as an indispensable adjunct to every house, great and small.

The effects of this movement, in a social sense, are likely to be far-reaching. It is probable that its influence, as levelling up the different ranks of society, will be for good. Town people will see more of country folk, and get to have a more accurate idea of the vital interests of the people at large. A cycling senator, being *incognito*, will very likely be able to form a more just idea of country problems than from studying the mere routine work and reports of his own district. There will be a more complete interchange of ideas, and a much greater knowledge of English beauties, than if just tearing from point to point in an express train. The great bugbear of late years has been centralisation, and this cycling seems inclined to counteract by the intermingling of people and the diffusion of ideas.

Some people appear to think that cycling owes its success to the fact that so many of the nobility have recognised its merits. Certainly they gave the sport a long, strong heave into notice; but for years, in a quiet way, cycling has been making its way amongst the most exclusive in the land. There were few big houses in the country that did not boast of a cycle, and the seed thus sown was bound to spring up sooner or later. If any one in particular gave a helping hand to cycling for ladies, it was Her Majesty the Queen. She grasped the possibilities for good in the *then* new idea, and by her prompt action in ordering a couple of machines in the earliest days, she hall-marked the movement, and to her the thanks of all cyclists are due.

That cycling in moderation can do much good becomes more and more evident every day. The exercise is an antidote to anæmia and other kindred disorders, due to our enervating style of living. Before cycling came to the rescue, it was by no means easy to get any exercise in London. Golf in town requires a good deal of energy and money, even to get to the nearest links. Tennis is by no means easily obtained. Walking is a very excellent way of getting a splitting headache, and the stifling air kills all desire for any other exercise than is unavoidable. Of course, cycling will at first be over-done—even with the best possible intentions on the part of its votaries. "The exercise is so delightful," the novice feels—and says—"she could go on for ever." Strolling round Regent's Park a short time ago, I passed a lady learning. She could go alone nicely, and was spinning along beside some others. "It is so glorious!" I heard her say, and it really seemed as if she meant what she said.

Now, the object of this little book is to give all needful advice on cycling, but there will be one warning throughout—the fruit of personal experience—*Be careful not to overdo it!*

2

Cycling Dress for Town and Country

IN THE OLD DAYS of tricycles, and when they were not at all the fashion, cycling dress was not the fine art it is now. Our only idea was to look neat, and be clad in weather-proof garments. Sailor hats in summer, and felt hats in autumn and winter, were the sum of elegance required, and fashions—Paris, rational and otherwise— did not require to be studied. We have changed all that now. If a tweed, serge, or homespun is worn, it must be of faultless cut, and cost as much as a riding-habit.

For park riding, we must have an artistically cut skirt, artfully arranged to hang in even portions each side of the saddle; and fashion decrees, what common-sense does not, that a blouse of silk or cotton, belaced, and with huge puff sleeves, is *en règle* for our bodies to be arrayed in. It very likely does not matter for the park in summer—these flimsy blouses,—though I should like to see how they looked after the rider had been caught in a shower of rain; but as to their being any good beyond Battersea Park and the Inner Circle, the idea is absurd.

Wool above, wool below, wool all over, such is the Medes and Persians hygienic rule for cycling. Cotton shirts for any long rides are, in an hygienic sense, impossible. They get damp, the rider stands about and rapidly begins to shiver, gets a bad chill and is laid up, when cycling gets the blame. In England, one can never be sure of the weather from day to day and hour to hour. Cyclists may start, and long in the morning, like Sydney Smith, to sit in their bones for coolness. Suddenly the wind gets round to north or east, and blowing through the damp cotton gives the rider the feeling of being cased in ice. This is no imaginary sketch. On the eastern coast of England I have often been metaphorically grilled one hour, and glad to get into a sealskin for warmth two or three hours later in the same day. The woollen undergarments may be light, or of substantial thickness, according to the personal idiosyncrasies of the wearer—but they must be wool. Several firms, I believe, make a speciality of cycling underwear. In many of the ladies' papers which now give cycling dress advice, one almost invariably sees cotton or openwork stockings recommended. Well, they may do for a few turns in the Row, but for anything more they would create a fine crop of blisters, and cause a tendency to sore feet which would prove exceedingly troublesome, not to say painful. Light woollen stockings to match the dress, unless gaiters—of which more anon—be worn, are best, and it is well to change them after riding. Whatever else is neglected, the feet must be kept in cool, hard condition, as if once they get into a bad state it is a long time ere they recover.

Some wise people say that corsets should be discarded for cycling. This is not correct. There should be no approach to tight-lacing, but a pair of woollen-cased corsets afford great support; they keep the figure from going all abroad, and protect the vital parts from chills. Special woollen-cased corsets are made by at any rate two manufacturers, who have spared no pains to provide a safe and good corset for cyclists.

It is essential in cycling to have well-cut knickerbockers in lieu of skirts. They can be obtained at most ladies' tailors, the price running to about £1. It is best to have them lined with leather as for riding on horseback. They

should be made to buckle at the knee, but loosely—
no tight bands are allowed in cycling. In the same
way, suspenders should invariably be used to secure the
stockings.

As I have mentioned before, cycling dress for town
and for country is quite a different thing. In town,
human nature must be fashionable, and—though it is not
hygienic—those riding in town must study the fashion of
the hour. It is not meant by this that riders are to adopt
the ridiculous blouses and flower-garden hats. These
are unmitigatedly absurd, and the worst possible style
for a pastime which demands, above all things, that the
rider should be neat, smart, and in harmony with the
workmanlike machine she rides. But there is no reason
why she need not call in light grey alpaca, white pique
and brown holland to form her coat and skirt. The days
of white facings are already past. They "caught on" with
the multitude, and their success proved their ruin. With
these light, summery materials, and the good taste and
cut of a trained *modiste*, cyclists can turn out so that it
is a pleasure to see them. Their costumes will not stand
wear, but those who ride in town can afford a change of
dress for different surroundings, therefore that considera-
tion need be no drawback. As a rule, the skirts in town
are much too wide. I was talking over this with a dress-
maker, and her explanation was it "looked so graceful,

the folds billowing out." Well, people have different views. This surplus of material very rarely *is* equally divided. In nine cases out of ten, it resembles the balloon jib of a yacht, and creates marvel in the mind how the rider escapes being wound up. To counteract this fault, the divided skirt has been introduced. The Pedaleuse is said to be the best of these, but nearly every tailor has his own speciality. Those who have the manufacturing of their own riding gear must bear in mind that no braid or flimsy lining is to appear on a cycling dress. There have been more serious accidents through these two adjuncts than through anything else. It is best for all-round riding to have the bottom of the skirt turned up a good six or eight inches, and this strongly stitched round with five or six rows of machine stitching. This stiffens and consolidates the hem. Another improvement is to have the skirt made to button each side, and no opening at the back at all in which the saddle peak can catch. It is a good plan to have a couple of elastic straps sewn firmly each side of the skirt, adjusted so that they do not drag or pull the dress out of hanging quite straight. These attach to buttons on gaiters, made to match the dress. Gaiters are needed, as the skirt for country and serious riding should be about down to the instep, and these short skirts, unless supplemented with spat gaiters, have an ugly unfinished look. Made in Harris tweed, homespun, serge, or Irish frieze, this costume is as good a one for all-round work as can be. It is neat and strong; rational, without being unladylike; safe, for if made with the turned-up hem there is nothing can catch; suitable alike for a country walk or ride, skating, or golf. The skirt should in no case exceed two and a half yards round, and the only lining should be a square of *glacé* silk over the knees, well away from the region of the pedals. Any good London firm will make a "common sense" dress on these lines, or a country tailor can do it. There is no complication or patent rights to run up the cost. The material should be good, so should be the cut and the stitching.

It is one of the commonest mistakes to read of boots being recommended for cycling in. They are utterly unsuitable, and should never be worn by any one who ever dreams of pedalling properly. Shoes, rationally made of brown or black leather, with plenty of room for the toes, are the right thing. And for cycling it is economy in the end to go to a good shoemaker, and get a hand-sewn shoe to fit the foot, instead of a pointed atrocity that the foot has to squeeze into, productive of endless pain and other evils. Brown leather, stained with a weak solution of coffee, to remove the hideous new look, is best for touring, being more easily cleaned. But they show so much, they must be well fitting and neat. Those who ride much will find a pair of rat-trap pedals, and grooved soles, the acme of comfort. These pedals do not improve the boot soles, it is true, but there is such a grip gained by their use, and delightful freedom from slipping, that those who really can ride will find them well deserving of the high character most good riders give them.

Hats and gloves are more a matter of taste than a hard and fast rule. Hat-pins should be avoided, and a band of broad elastic or velvet put to keep them on. There are few things to beat a good sailor hat for neatness and comfort in summer riding. A felt is best for winter. Gloves are an open question: dark ventilated tan look nice and wear well; white doeskin are fairly good and fashionable; white kid are absurd and extortionate for a sport like cycling. Silk and cotton soon wear into holes and are extremely hot, not to mention that they blister the hands they are meant to protect. Handknitted wool ones are best for cold and rainy weather.

Collars and ties are smart and do well for short cool rides. The shirts with detachable collars, to be had at any ladies' shirt tailor, are extremely neat and useful.

Veils are a questionable advantage: they keep the hair tidy in windy weather, also providing a protection against flies in the eyes; but to muffle up in a blue or white thick gauze, as some do, is not only absurd but also suffocating. It is said they are a protection against sunburn, but most sensible riders would prefer to get a little wholesome tan, to going about with their heads in a semi-opaque bag.

Country riding dress must be weather-proof, capable of standing and warding off a shower, and taking no harm from a thorough drenching. To all of us a wet ride comes sooner or later, and so long as the rider is clad in wool, and keeps moving, there is no danger of catching cold.

3
About Machines

THE STOCK question of every one about to begin cycling is always, "Which is the best machine?" and inquirers are much surprised to be told that there is not one best, but half-a-dozen or more. For fashion, finish, design, and price, the Humber and Elswick stand perhaps first in the field, the latter being beyond all doubt the best thought-out machine in the market, and a Beeston Humber is, as a Lincolnshire man would put it, "very bad to beat." But at the same time, for touring and general work, the Coventry Machinists, with their Swifts; J. K. Starley, with the Rover; the Singer Co., with the De Luxe; the Raleigh, Premier, Osmond, Ivel, and Sunbeam cycles; the machines of the Rudge-Whitworth Co., Humber & Co., and Marriott & Cooper;—all of these makes are first-rate, reliable, and capable of doing everything the rider can want. There are now so many makers that it is to specialities that we must look. Some build ladies' machines of extra lightness, others of special strength for rough work; some, like the Rovers, are ideal for touring; the Singers are famed for their excellent material; the Swifts for their close, compact build; the Premiers for their rigidity and helical tube;—so that any one asking the question at the head of this chapter will see how difficult it is to answer it fairly.

"I do not want to give much," is another qualification which opens the door for those death-traps, "cheap" machines. A good machine can very seldom be had for little money, especially now that there is so great a run on them. The general public want light and strong bicycles with pneumatic tyres and every improvement for from £7 to £10. A good light machine is the most expensive of all, because it needs flawless tube, and skilled work to make the junctions. People are a great deal too apt to gauge the price of a machine by the beauty of its enamel and plating. In reality, the money value of the whole cycle lies in the bearings. The ball-bearings in cheap machines are so only in name. The steel is soft and wears into irregular grooves, and the pleasure of riding on a machine in such a state is rather of the negative order. Those who want to know all about the working mechanism of their machines should study a good handbook on the subject, and avail themselves of every opportunity of making a practical application of the knowledge thus gained. They will then feel less surprise why all good machines are so high priced.

But because a machine is not a Humber or a Rover, it by no means follows that it is good for nothing. Many small country makers turn out excellent machines at from £14 to £16. But when buying of a local or unknown maker, it is best to take an experienced friend to aid in the choice. It is a well-known fact that any brilliantly plated contrivance is good enough for a lady—in the vendor's estimation; what the bearings are like she is not supposed to know—or care about.

A very light machine is a great mistake. The American machines are excellent for park and easy wear, but for a rough road in the country they would be extremely un-comfortable, even if they stood the continued jolting. As

I have said before, if a machine is light (26 lbs.) it must be very well made. This entails skilled workmen, who cannot, and will not, work for nothing; the light gauge-tube must be faultless—another expense; and when all is said and done, when it comes to touring with luggage, and riding over all sorts of roads, it is most likely that the machine will run much heavier than an ordinary roadster weighing 32 lbs.

The shapes of frames are divided into two classes—the angular straight-tubed frame and the double-curved tubes. The single-curved tube has had its day; fashionable people liked it because of the dress clearance, but no single tube can stand the strain which centres above the crank-bracket. Singer and Starley Brothers held on for a long time, but I believe that both make double-tube frames now. For touring abroad, the strongest machine in the market is the patent triangulated frame, made by Humber & Co. In this the angle strain is met just where it is greatest by two bracing tubes, and the machine is as stiff and rigid as that of a man's. Another very strong frame is the Raleigh; this has a duplex angle-tube to the steering head in front, which is immensely strong.

Handle-bars are best if of the plain, flat-fronted, curved type. Those twisted and contorted like a ram's horn are not only very difficult to repair, but give the impression of a bath-chair guiding-handle. When set

high they are beyond measure hideous, and it is impossible to pull at them when a hill or bit of rough ground
renders such assistance of use, though, as a general rule,
all pulling should be reduced to a minimum.

The handle-grips themselves are best made of cork.
If they are washed occasionally with ordinary household
soap they can easily be kept clean. They are cooler and
cleaner than felt.

Pedals are of two sorts—the rat-trap, and those with
the thick bars of rubber or felt. The latter are considered
the best for ladies' use, but the comfort of fitted shoes
and the steel rat-trap pedals is so great, that for all who
mean real riding I cordially recommend them. The
shoes worn should have a special sole, rather broad in
the welt, to protect the leather from the friction of the
steel side-plates. The rider should put her foot square on
the pedal, in the position used when riding, and get the
shoemaker to mark with chalk where the slits should be
left. He should then put on another rather light sole in
pieces, being careful that it is well pegged or sewn where
the slits occur—not only round the edge. When done,
the grip is something enormous, yet the foot is in no way
fettered as with toe-clips, which should on no account
be used by ladies, as they are most dangerous friends.

Tyres seem to be almost universally Dunlops, yet the
Clincher is extremely good, and the Palmer has many

adherents. For ladies' machines I should recommend as the best possible the Scottish; the Fleuss is also very good. The chief beauty of the Scottish is the perfect ease with which the outer cover can be taken off. It is not easy to get the wire of a Dunlop over the rim, even when one knows, both theoretically and practically, how it is done. There is a fancy just now to put a non-slipping cover on the back wheel, and a plain, smooth cover on the front. For the country this arrangement answers well enough, but in town I have found the tendency to side-slip much increased by it. It is best, therefore, to be on the safe side, and insist on having non-slippers to both back and front wheels.

The argument in favour of a plain front cover is that it is less injured by the brake. Certainly a brake does grind down the non-slipping tyre a little, but the danger of side-slip is worth the expenditure of another pound a year to replace the damaged part. Some meet the difficulty by dispensing with the brake itself. Now, granting that a brake sometimes damages the tyre, it is yet so important an adjunct that no woman should dream of riding without one. A novice has not the power in her ankles to hold a machine in down a bad hill with anything approaching safety. People think it smart to say airily, "I never use a brake!" It may be a new light to them to make the obvious retort that they cannot have ridden much, or must be both reckless of their own lives and those of other people. There is no need to jam on a brake for every little hill, but in touring one may be on a hill of unknown steepness at any moment. Not only must every machine have a brake, but the brake must be both powerful and easy to apply. The pneumatic brake is, on the whole, said to be very good, but the best lever-brake is the Roper brush, which checks the tyre without injuring it. The Smith friction wheel-brake is also excellent; it is applied by the ordinary lever, and does not wear out the tyre cover. The most satisfactory lever-brake I have ever used was on a Humber. The lever was long, well-fitted, and cranked at the end to relieve the strain of the hand. Much more attention should be paid to this adjunct on the part of both riders and makers.

Saddles, also, are a weak point in a lady's machine. It is next to impossible to give reliable advice concerning them. Henson's and Burgess's saddles are good, but require the riders to be low and far back—so the knee-action becomes unpleasantly pronounced. Brookes' B85 and B302 are good saddles, *if well adjusted* with their patent saddle tilt. It will repay the rider to spend some time raising and lowering the saddle, tilting it backwards and forwards, till the most comfortable angle is obtained. It is quite possible to ride comfortably on an ordinary saddle, but it is not easy just at once to hit upon the correct position.

When choosing a first machine it is best to get one which is good and simple. Leave wonderful new ideas and gears alone. *Apropos* of this latter point, nine out of ten ladies' machines are geared far too low, sixty inches being none too high for a competent rider. Slow pedalling is much less exhausting than the chasing of feet round and round that goes on with a low gear. With good roads and average strength, sixty-five is not at all impossible. A gear-case, either a Carter or a Grose, should be used, not only because it keeps the chain from the dress, but because it protects it from mud and dirt, which is apt to be thrown back from the front wheel. If any one doubts their use, the state of the crank-brackets after a muddy run will bear a silent witness to the fact. In the same way mud-guards must be strong and good. In very muddy weather a piece of leather fastened to the bottom of the front mud-guard protects the feet and cranks, even if the road be deep in liquid mud. Any cycle agent will put one on for a shilling, and from experience I can vouch for the comfort thus gained.

A lamp and bell form important adjuncts to a machine. The Silver King, at 12*s*. 6*d*., is one of the best and worth double the price, being a most excellent lamp. The 20th Century, burning paraffin, is also good; it is made in aluminium as well as the usual metals. Electric lamps are a somewhat costly novelty, but should the rider be near a place where they can be recharged, they act well for a limited number of hours. With regard to bells, a rather large, deep-toned single strike gong clears the road better than the ordinary weary tinkle. Cyclometers add to the interest of a ride. The best and most scientific is the Boy's and Rücker, which rings a bell at every mile. The price is £1 1*s.* The Standard is tolerably reliable, as also are the Trenton and the tiny Veedor. On a long ride it is a great amusement to check the distances done. These three last cost from 5*s.* to 10*s.* each.

One of the most valuable adjuncts to a cycling household is a Hutton cycle-stand and stand-pump. They can be had either separately or combined, the price of the latter at the Army and Navy Stores being 14*s.* A plain foot-pump, with connecting screws to fit any make of tyre, can be got for 10*s.* By its means tyres can be inflated with great ease, and a frequent cause of punctures— riding with a slack tyre—is thus avoided.

A cycle lock is frequently very useful when visiting at houses, or when staying at hotels abroad. So many are made that it is easy to choose one. The letter lock cycle-clasps are specially good.

The Martin Silent tool-bag is a recent invention. Its speciality is a small bit of undetachable felt, in which the spanners are enveloped. There are many other tool-bags renowned for excellence. A watch-holder is a dubious blessing. Under no circumstances should a good watch be trusted on such a centre of vibration as a handle-bar. If any be used, the commonest Waterbury is quite good enough to spoil in this fashionable manner.

4

How to Ride
and How Not to Ride

It ought to be the exception, not the rule, to see a bad rider in the present day. So much has been said, so much has been written, so many (to quote a favourite saying of our parents) have had the best masters and the greatest advantages money can purchase; yet, strange to say, a really good rider is as much a *rara avis* as ever. Perhaps, although the instructions are excellent, they are not read; be the master ever so good, his teaching goes in at one ear and out at the other; or it may be the native contrariety of the race which leads us, one and all, to do just what we ought not to do—at any rate, many of the present race of cyclists have much to learn before they win their spurs as good riders.

I have an idea that readers, after perusing the above jeremiad, will inquire curiously: What is good riding, then? It is generally understood to be an entire want of effort, and an harmonious swing. The rider and her machine move as one; fast or slow, rough or smooth, whatever the road, the good rider sails along, apparently effortless as a hawk on the wing. Her knees do *not* pump up and down as if belonging to a donkey-engine; the arms are *not* extended in a semicircle at right angles to the body; but the whole effect is that of a continuation of the machine, and the two form a pleasant picture. The bad rider is all angles. If she reads a book which tells her to sit high, she contrives to "guy" the whole thing. She gets so high she can just follow round the pedals with a kind of sewing-machine motion; her back is crooked and constrained, and there is a want of ease and continuity about the whole which is very painful to the eye of the looker-on. It is a modern development this bad riding, this sitting high. Learners are told that they must sit high, and with the best intentions in life, but with an utter lack of reasoning power, they ride as much too high as their greatly maligned sisters formerly rode too low in Battersea Park.

The right position is a happy medium. The rider must be about an inch to an inch and a half within her "reach." This allows room for ankle action, which is a *sine qua non* in good riding. Learners may be lower at first, but it must be a clearly understood thing that as they gain confidence the saddle must be gradually raised to the height before mentioned. Then the backward and forward shifting must be taken into account. There is a great deal said about the discomfort of nearly all saddles, but in nine cases out of ten proper adjusting makes a marvellous difference in ease of riding. A great many people seem quite unable to use a spanner or wrench with any degree of facility. In the early days of riding, the "King Dick" wrench—on the whole the best made—should be kept in the coat pocket, and should be used till comfort is obtained. The seat pillar always adjusts by slackening the nut at the top of the enamelled tube. I have heard some ladies remark, "I don't think my seat will move—there's no screw." It is a case of no eyes in this instance. Every machine, bad or good, can have its saddle raised or lowered, and most saddles have tilts to allow of alteration in slope. Every bicycle should have this movement fitted.

Once the saddle is got right, the handles must be adjusted. As a rule, a shade higher than the peak of the saddle is about right, but a great deal depends on length of arms, height, etc. The upcurved handles should always, when possible, be discarded, and the plain, flat-fronted bar put in their place. Apart from their absurdity, and the idiotic position they entail on the user, the former shape, by requiring to be leant on and gripped, conveys a large amount of vibration to the rider, which is far better dispensed with.

Once the machine is properly adjusted, and the rider has confidence—both in herself and her mount—she is far up the stair which leads to success. Many find mounting and dismounting a bugbear. The best way is to slant the machine a tiny bit towards the rider, who then gets into the frame. The mounting knee should be well bent, almost reaching the foot-rest on the front fork; the hands rest on the handles. When ready the knee is simply straightened, the machine gathers way and moves forward, lifting the rider into the saddle by the movement of straightening the knee. The pedal should be nearly upright—quite so if the machine has short cranks. Some mount with the right foot, others with the left. This is a mere question of taste, but it is best to practise with both. Beginners may give a slight kick to start themselves, but when in practice it is quite easy to step on the raised pedal and swing off without hopping, or other jarring movement. The hideous fashion of sitting low on the machine and then kicking off with one leg must be discarded by every one who dreams of riding at all well. Not only is it ugly, it is dangerous.

Mistakes are often made about pedalling. There are various styles: the steam-pump action, already alluded to; instep pedalling, peculiar to the learner; and the exaggerated ankle action which has lately become somewhat common in the park. The first is simply waste of labour. One foot works against the other, and it is small wonder if those practising it find cycling hard work. Instep pedalling is very tiresome to combat. It has the drawback of entirely checking all ankle action. It also looks bad, and is really harder work, necessitating, as it does, a low seat, but learners say it gives them a feeling of confidence, and it almost needs the patience of a saint to get them to use the fore part of the foot. In good action the muscles of the foot all unite in pushing one pedal forward, and at the same time in pulling the other one back—so causing a circular motion of the feet—and utilising every atom of power. The technical name is "clawing." The toes wind round the pedal bar and grip them almost as the hand holds the boss of a brace in drilling. There is not a dead weight on either pedal, but a nervous intelligent grip of the bars which enables a spurt to be made by the action of dropping the heels and tightening every muscle of the foot and ankle. By means of this method of pedalling complete control is gained over the machine. The weight of the body aids by being distributed over the saddle and pedals, not all bearing on the former. Steering becomes much easier when it is more a question of varying pressure on the pedals than gripping at the steering bar. This is the secret of riding well. A practised rider can steer as well without the handles as with them, a feat that the "steam-pump action" rider will lamentably fail in.

To pedal properly, it is best to use rat-trap pedals and fitted shoes. They have drawbacks—in tearing the shoes and rusting easily,—but if the shoes are properly made, with slits in the soles, by a good shoemaker, there is really little damage done. If rubber pedals are used, the shoes should also be fitted so as to grip them by means of an extra sole with wider slots. In wet or very dusty weather the tendency of rubber pedals to slip is marked, and a slippery pedal is not only tiresome but dangerous.

Most people, as soon as they can keep their balance, demonstrate their proficiency by sweeping round every corner at the most rapid pace they can compass. This is not wise. It may look smart, but when, as often happens, side-slip occurs, the machine going one way and the rider the other, then the game is hardly worth the candle. In muddy weather, and *very dry dusty* weather, it is highly advisable to take corners, and even to ride on a well raised road, with caution. Besides, no one can tell what obstacle may be round a sharp corner, and if there is much pace on it is impossible to pull up short. More will be said on this subject in the next chapter, but, as a general rule, the best riders are the most careful. Hill-climbing is essentially the fruit of good practice—knack, and ankle action. In this, as in riding in a head wind, it is slow persistence which scores. To attempt to take a long hill at a charging pace is absolutely absurd and hurtful. The best way, supposing the road is a steady upgrade, is to sit down in the saddle and go up slowly. The body need not be bent into a bow, but should be upright with a slight bend forwards. The ankle and calf muscles must do the work between them. When the rise needs frantic tugs at the handles, and causes the breath to come in gasps, then it ought to be walked. It is a great mistake to ride every hill, even if it be a moderate one. Some days it may be possible to do hills easier than on others, but when the effort becomes in the least severe the rider will be far better walking.

It may be taken as a general rule that few hills are worth riding unless they can be done easily. To strain and push, as many do, is most harmful. But all the same, by practice and knack, very stiff grades can be taken without the least distress. The chief factors of success are ankle action and a steady persevering swing.

In going down hill, it is by no means necessary to wear the tyre out prematurely by excessive braking. The brake is an adjunct to back pedalling, not to be either entirely discarded, or entirely relied on. Ladies should not fly down hills feet up. On a tricycle it was perfect, but on a bicycle the danger outweighs the advantage. It is best to keep the machine in check, at a uniform steady swing, till the road is seen to be clear, and then let on pace, but never so as to lose control over the machine. It is unwise in every sense to depend on back pedalling alone, if for no other reason than the extremely insecure junction of the chain links. Serious accidents are constantly happening from the chain giving way, and for this reason, if for no other, a reliable brake should always be fitted *and used*.

5

Riding in Towns

TO RIDE SAFELY in a town, especially where there is any considerable traffic, is a development of cycling which should only be attempted by those who are thoroughly at home on their wheels, and who are gifted with cool heads and strong nerves. Even when the rider has all these advantages, the most crowded streets are best avoided so far as may be. Putting aside the question as to whether it is quite nice for ladies to run alone

34

the gauntlet of the vulgar chaff sometimes hurled at them—from whichever point it is looked at, lady riders are best out of traffic. The question was recently put: "Should or should not ladies cycle in London streets?" and the answers were decidedly against their doing so.

If, from circumstances over which the lady rider has no control, she has a valid reason for town riding, the following hints may be of service. Concentrate your mind on the work in hand, keep the eyes looking steadily straight ahead, the heels down, and the machine under the most perfect control. Be ready to stop almost dead; to signal to the carriages behind, by the outstretched left hand, when a check occurs in the line of traffic. Avoid showy dashes, swoops, and narrow shaves under horses' noses and between vehicles. Slacken speed at cross streets; listen carefully for the sound of anything coming; even in the turmoil of London hearing is a great help, though some may say that in such a din one noise more or less cannot be noticed. In town riding the ears become educated after a little to the song of the traffic, and can distinguish differences in a most marvellous manner.

The cardinal rule in riding in England is "keep to the left," all vehicles to be passed on the right. This needs to be more generally understood and observed, for nothing worries and irritates a driver more than bicyclists who will go their wrong side. But by keeping to the left is not meant keeping right in to the kerbstone. Most town streets slope on each side, and it is highly important to keep on or about the crown of the causeway. A rider who keeps too far in by the kerb is apt to be hustled and jammed by traffic passing on the right, in a way which none but the strongest nerves can stand. The proper place for a cycle is in the line of traffic to the left side of the road. Once there, it should be borne in mind that in the eye of the law a cycle is a carriage—entitled to the same privileges and subject to the same penalties. So long as the rider remembers this, observes the rules of the road, and behaves with ordinary courtesy, there should be no friction. There are many who receive most courteous treatment from 'bus drivers, carmen, and cabmen; but there are others who seem to act as a cycling nettle, and are always in hot water. In plain English, if the great rules of courtesy, and give and take, are observed, no lady need complain of insolence on the part of the often much aggravated drivers in the streets of our large towns.

Side-slip is an evil which is at present but very unsatisfactorily combated. For town riding non-slipping tyres are a certain safeguard, but in most cases the difficulty is due to nervousness and unequal pedalling. On a day when the roads are very greasy—either from copious deluges from watering-carts or heavy showers—it is as well to lower the saddle a little. The thrust of the foot is thus lessened, and the rider's centre of gravity is lower. Under slippery conditions the pace should be a steady swing, easing down almost to walking pace when taking corners. It is somewhat odd that two utterly different conditions cause acute side-slip—very dusty roads and muddy ones. On a quite wet day in London, on the wood pavement, the running will be as firm as can be; the rain has swept the grease off, and the worn wood gives an excellent hold. But on a very dusty day—either in town or country—even non-slipping tyres are no use. One of the worst falls I ever had was caused by side-slip on a dusty drive entrance.

In Gloucestershire, Oxfordshire, and parts of Wiltshire, a horrible geological mixture termed oolite is found. When wet—either much or little—it becomes as slippery as the greased ways of a shipbuilder's yard. Care will enable the rider to keep upright, but it requires a good deal of this, and perfectly even pedalling. In this last item lies the secret of safe riding.

This, by the way, is a digression from my immediate subject, but side-slip and how to avoid it is a most important matter. Among the many evil devices of the builders of towns, tram-lines unquestionably are the worst. To keep out of the street they mar by their presence is the best advice, but if obliged to ride among them, be most particular always to cross at an acute angle. To take them with a slight deviation from the straight is just an invitation to a bad fall. The machine must be headed straight at them, either at right angles, or at as acute an angle as possible, and only straightened up when the last line is crossed by the hind wheel. Riding in a tram-line is very unsafe. The same advice also applies to the stone sets which often form a distinct ridge in the road; these also must be taken at a sharp angle.

In crossing stone sets, such as pathways over streets, it strains the machine far less if the rider stands up on her pedals, instead of sitting a dead weight in the saddle. The same applies to bumpy wood or macadam roads, which knock a machine to pieces, and give considerable discomfort to the rider. Sewer gratings must also be watched for. It is wonderful how many traps for the unwary the streets of the most civilised towns contain. In town riding, it is wisest not to attempt to show off, by riding with hands off, and trying other cheap tricks. It is taken for granted that every one can steer in suitable places with their feet, but display of such a nature in a crowded thorough-fare is not only dangerous—it is in bad taste.

Possibly in all towns riders have a standard trial in the shape of undecided pedestrians. Try as one may, sometimes a specimen comes across one's path who, no doubt unintentionally, tries to get across with a vigour worthy of a better cause. The offender generally stands on one side of the street and surveys right and left; the bicyclist rings her bell; and instead of the pedestrian waiting until the cyclist has passed, or coolly walking across, she gives a spasmodic run forward. Were it continued it would be all right, but in a trice it is changed to a rapid retrogression. Then ensue *pirouettes* on the part of the walker, and wobbles on the part of the rider. The end is, either the rider jumps off to avoid a tumble, or the undecided pedestrian comes into collision with the machine.

Now, people have no business to tear full speed down a crowded thoroughfare, but, at the same time, some pedestrians treat cyclists as if they had no right to exist at all. It is only reasonable to expect them to treat the cycle bell with the same attention as a rubber-tyred hansom's jinglers. Cyclists can generally avoid a decided person, but the one portrayed above is most trying.

Abroad, the rule of the road is "Keep to the right." In towns, as with us, it is forbidden (*défendu*) to ride on the footpath, or even to wheel a machine thereon. It is forbidden to sweep round corners at full speed, the penalty varying from five to fifteen francs. Riders are in all cases required to carry a lamp. In France and, I believe, Germany, the cyclist has to carry a plate with either number or name and address, full particulars of which can be had at the London offices of the C.T.C. Towns abroad are generally paved with the most bone-shaking stone sets, which, in most cases, are better walked. When to these is added an electric tramway, as at Montreux, on the Lake of Geneva, then cyclists must be on their guard.

Sudden stoppages of carts, etc., also carts sweeping round broadside on, when riding in traffic, are most productive of accidents; in the latter case the cyclist is apt to ride into the revolving wheel. These dangers may be guarded against by having the machine well in hand, and being able to ride slowly. An out-stretched left hand will always check traffic behind. A look-out must be kept in front for a raised hand, or whip straight upright, being the "block signal" used by all drivers.

Crossings of main streets are best taken riding slowly till a sight can be obtained both ways. When a gap appears, a sharp touch of the bell will call drivers' attention, and room will be made for her to cross. If nervous, or it is a bad crossing, like Regent Circus or by the Marble Arch, it is wisest, if not most dignified, to jump off.

6

Touring at Home
and Abroad

IT IS TO TOURING, not to fashion, that cycling owes most of its popularity. Steadily, from year to year, more and more people have adopted cycling in preference to pedestrianism as a means of seeing the country in the brief autumn vacation, which means new life to many a wearied town worker. Men and women now toil alike. The days are past when men alone provided the necessary labour in trade and profession; now, day by day, fresh fields of work are being opened, and women in many cases share the honour of being supports of the house. If they work, as thousands do, in close stuffy offices, bending over correspondence and accounts, type-writing, and in other sedentary employments, it is only fair that they should have an equal chance of fresh air with the men,—this is what makes touring on cycles so valuable for all classes of women, and this also is the cause, far more than any fashion, which has given cycling its present position among women. Possibly nothing is more appreciated by any rider than week-end tours—otherwise Saturday to Monday runs. It is so nice to get away from the stifling town for the Sunday, and spend it with friends in some country place, returning to town quite refreshed early on Monday morning. The baggage requisite for such outings can easily be carried on the cycle, even to a full change of dress, though it requires a little judgment, both in choosing one which will be light, suitable, elegant, and at the same time stand crushing well. I shall make very few suggestions on this point. Every woman has different ideas on dress, and it would be waste of space to prescribe special toilets.

Roughly speaking, a light silk or crepon skirt and a silk blouse are ideal touring change dress. The riding dress should be of light cloth or covert coating, the coat built so that with a detachable front it can be worn off the machine on Sunday in conjunction with the crepon skirt. Hats are a puzzle. A "sailor" is neatness itself, but not by any means dressy, and the addition of a flower-garden hat would be the plague of the rider's life. Either the riding hat must be made to serve, or the best hat be sent on securely packed by parcel post, and very often the same medium will take the dress also, and deliver it in time to be worn.

The things which must be carried are an entire change of woollen underwear. There is nothing worse than standing about in damp clothes, and the luxury of a bath and change after a hot dusty ride must be experienced to be believed in. Under no circumstances, therefore, must this change be omitted. A brush and comb, tooth brush, sponge, tiny cake of soap, change of shoes and stockings, housewife with mending tackle, and a map of the route—all these are absolutely necessary. It is best for riders to carry some brandy and Eau-de-Cologne—especially in hot weather—also a small box of vestas. Outside these, the rider must judge for herself and consult her own comfort and needs. A few trips will give her a practical object-lesson in making herself as comfortable as possible; as people have varying ideas on this subject, it is not needful to give a table of trifles, and as space is limited I shall proceed to the touring machine.

There is no good object served in having a machine for this sort of work too light. As I have explained before, a light machine is either very costly, or unable to stand rough roads, luggage-carrying, and general use. A machine of 30 lbs. is none too heavy, and can be used by even slightly-built riders. Freedom in running is far more important than actual lightness. Care should be taken to see that the handles are on a broad, flat-fronted bar; that the brake-lever is long, cranked upwards, and powerful; that the rubber lining to the spoon is all right; the wheels true; the tyres either fitted with self-closing air tubes, or strong ordinary ones; the tool bag should be overhauled; the oil-can carefully filled; if a "King Dick" adjustable wrench is not a part of the outfit it should be added, together with a lock and chain; and a long pump should be carried, attached *with straps* up the seat pillar. Straps will be found infinitely better than clips, as they do not injure either the enamel or the pump, and if turned once round the seat pillar before being fastened round the pump they obviate all cause for rattle.

It follows also, as a matter of course, that a tyre repairing outfit must be carried, and the owner must know how to use it in mending any punctures which may happen to the tyres.

As in a machine for touring everything must be good, workmanlike, and simple, so also should be the dress. It must be borne in mind that an ideal touring dress must be built to look equally well both on and off the machine. This is far too often neglected. Most people want to leave their machines at their stopping-places and explore on foot. This is easy enough if they are in a quiet, well-cut, tailor-made dress, which may be somewhat short—in these golfing days no one notices that. As to head wind, and hampering skirts, and the thousand and one flimsy objections of the rational dress school, their fallacy has been demonstrated over and over again. Head winds are a plague, whether walking, riding, cycling, driving, or skating; the only way to manage in cycling is to reduce the pace to a steady plod, and not try to fight the wind.

The choice of material and style is a matter for every one to settle for themselves. The dress should be capable of throwing off a shower, and all linings and bands should be of woollen material. Any of the official tailors of the C.T.C. will show a selection of approved cloths and styles at moderate prices. Irish frieze is admirable for its weather-proof qualities, and so is Harris tweed. Perhaps for general usefulness the coat and skirt style is best with a front or waistcoat or skirt. The Norfolk jacket style is also good, when well made. As to gaiters for touring, I should personally be very sorry to dispense with them. Shoes are a *sine qua non*, and walking up hill, when the roads are loose and dusty, the grit enters by the lace holes, and is apt, by the grinding action set up, to cause sore feet. The gaiters also protect the feet from the stings of the tiny "thunder flies," which often cause so much swelling of the feet as to lame the rider. *Apropos* of flies, boracic acid lotion is a very good thing for bites, as well as cuts or bruises. It is cheap and non-poisonous, and a small bottle or even packet of crystals is a very handy addition to the touring kit. The right strength is 1 oz. crystals, 25 oz. water.

Those desiring to take extended tours at home or abroad should join the Cyclists' Touring Club for England, and the Touring Club de France for the Continent. Information regarding the latter can be had from the C.T.C. offices. Not only do the members of the C.T.C. have the privilege of free entry to French ports, but in every English town there is a Consul to whom to apply for information on routes and roads. There are hotels which cater for members at reduced charges, and there is a special magazine issued free, monthly, to all Club members. The Club is also establishing special facilities for lady members in the shape of Lady Consuls in each large town, to whom to refer in the event of tourists falling ill, or meeting with accidents far away from their own people. There is also in course of formation a country lodgings and farmhouse list, so that members who do not care to spend their holidays riding along the roads can choose country centres, from which they can explore the country, golf, sketch, photograph, or rest absolutely. The Club appoints qualified repairers in each town, who have to give proof of their competence to repair machines, and, finally, publish the "Handbook," one of the most exhaustive cycling publications in England; it is also in course of publishing a detailed and accurate road-book.

Touring at home is one thing, touring abroad another. It is more pleasant, but also more necessary, to have an official ticket to show, and a powerful organisation at one's back. To the cyclist, her C.T.C. ticket, and a passport, are almost indispensable abroad. To a foreigner a *billet* for everything is a part of his being, and the Briton who ignores the "rubbishy tags of paper" will find out that when abroad it is best to put that and other insular prejudices in his or her pocket.

It is highly important that ladies especially should only go moderate distances at first; any day's work over forty miles is too much. Most like a tour to do them good, and these should exercise scrupulous self-restraint in distance. Dine simply but well, start early, and rest during the heat of the day, having an *al fresco* lunch if the weather permits. A hobby of some sort, either a sketch-book or a camera, is a great help to taking an excursion easily. So also is a pursuit, such as archæology, botany, photography. The route required should be carefully studied, and a good-sized map carried. Short cuts should be avoided. A compass should be carried, as it is often a great help when touring, especially in flat countries where landmarks are few. We English are only just awaking to the fact that our crazy sign-posts are a national disgrace beside the useful ones of enamelled iron used abroad.

In touring, when thirsty, drink milk and soda, with a biscuit, if possible. The cheap teetotal drinks are dangerous. Good "stone-ware" ginger beer is safe, but as a rule the commercial ginger beer is not good. Egg beaten up in milk, with a teaspoonful of whisky, is excellent when a rider is at all done up. Shandygaff, if made of good materials, is valuable. There are so few facilities for getting anything to drink in a country ride, say, on the Westmorland Fells or the Lincolnshire Wolds, that it is generally best to carry a flask of claret and water, or some equally sound beverage, and be safe and independent. Milk alone, when taken in quantities, *is dangerous, if the rider be very hot.*

7

Hill-Climbing

IN THE OLD DAYS, when tricycles were looked on as uncanny creations, not altogether as respectable as they might be, one problem exercised many people's minds, and that was hills. Going down them could be understood by the general public; but "How do you manage when you come to an ascent?" The natural reply that moderate hills could be ridden up, and other, steeper ones, could be walked, caused a dubious shake of the head. People, it was easy to see, had not much idea of our veracity in pretending to go up hill on "those things," and even now—ten years later—hill-climbing on cycle-back is still regarded with much more respect than it really deserves.

Now, there are hills and hills. I have known long gradual "grinds" which to the uninitiated looked stretches of level road, and these have taken as much steady work as even a steep "danger-board hill." For very shame one cannot get off on what is practically level road, yet every stroke shows that the grade is there, though owing to the nature of the road it does not show. With a steady head wind a stretch of this sort is one of the most tiring things a cyclist can encounter.

Take another kind—one of the orthodox switchback order—a regular V in shape, but having what hunting men call "a good take-off," a showy sort of hill to ride, just the kind to impress a wavering admirer of the wheel. Coming to the brink and sitting well back in the saddle, with the brake just touching—swish! away goes the rider, letting go about half-way down to allow the momentum to have its full effect in scaling the other side,—then, with a dig of the pedals and a pull at the handles, the wheel is sent flying up. There is a stiff bit at the top, but the rider has swing and momentum to help, so with a few vigorous claws at the pedals she is up and over the brink, sailing away on level road. This is a showy hill, and requires only nice judgment and skill to get up it, not much strength.

Another sort, which is most tiresome to manage, is when the hill begins to swell up ahead, and look much worse than when the rider started. When I encounter a hill like this on a ride, in nine cases out of ten it is walked, and generally, when viewed from above, it can be seen to be a long steady grade with a sudden steepening at the top—the worst sort of hill to manage. Hill-climbing is a combination of strength and knack. The good climber will know that it is far more important to utilise the weight and the ankle muscles than to bend the body in form of a crescent, and thus pull, puff, and strain, in all probability injuring herself and not succeeding half as well as if she had gone to work quietly. Some hills can be rushed—like the "showy switchback one" quoted before,—railway bridges and canal bridges, stiff hummocky bits which still disgrace some country roads. But the best way to take a long hill is to go slowly, not to rush up full speed till it is impossible to go on any further, but to ease up at the bottom and deliberately begin the ascent, sitting quite upright, with a slight pull at the handles now and then, but no crouching or straining. The ankle muscles must do the work; they must keep both pedals working one in with the other.

The toes must do their part in forcing one set of pedal bars forward, whilst those on the other foot hook them backward, and so on, round and round, just as the crank rod carries round the huge driving wheels of the Great Northern express engines.

It is slow and sure that does the business. The hill may be a steep one, but the rider who knows her work should forge ahead, not breathless and panting, but breathing quietly and easily, never spurting, never hurrying, but keeping up the steady, uniform swing. Then, when the top is reached and all strain removed, she dashes ahead as fresh, and breathing as steadily, as if she had been on the level all along. Such is scientific hill-climbing—steadiness, using the weight to assist the ankles in their perfect revolution. A bad rider would go at the same hill head down—pulling at the handles, pumping with her feet—working one crank against the other—pushing, puffing, straining every nerve, and arriving at the top dishevelled and hopelessly exhausted.

One thing the maligned tricycles taught the old riders, and that was how to ride hills. Pushing a heavy 70 lb. machine up north-country "banks" was a good training school. Last autumn I was over the old familiar ground on a light bicycle and came across a towering hill, which in old days I had ridden on a heavy tricycle. To be sure, by the time I had conquered the "bank," the backbone of my machine was severely sprung; but in the autumn sunshine last year I stood beside my light Humber bicycle and asked myself how I had contrived to ride that hill on a heavy tricycle ten years before. I tried to repeat the feat on the bicycle, but failed absolutely and absurdly a sixth of the way up.

Some people say that all hills should be walked. This is nonsense. One expects cyclists to bring to bear in hill-climbing the same common-sense as in other things. If a hill involves too much exertion, get off. On the contrary, if a steep hill is taken steadily, it is little more exertion than to walk up, wheeling the machine. It is no use trying to force the pace, either up hill or against a head wind. It is slowness and steadiness wins, not paltry spurts.

Tacking across a hill, as a Devonshire pony does, in some cases makes the work easier, but if the road is at all a frequented one these tacks—"glorified wobbles"—must be avoided. Personally, I have never found any great benefit from such action.

Hill-climbing is a safe and pleasant amusement compared to the manifold dangers of carelessness down hill—from no cause have there been so many accidents. In no way is folly of the most idiotic character so abundantly shown as in the recklessness of novices down hill—in their disregard of the absolute necessity

of having adequate brake power. I should recommend
either a proper brush or a pneumatic brake to be fixed to
every machine in a hilly country; the latter is excellent
if held as a reserve power, fitted to a back wheel. The
lever should be strong and well fitted, so that it does not
strain the hand. Too little attention has in the past been
paid to this matter.

8
Bicycle Gymkhanas

THE BICYCLE has come out in many curious lights,
but not the least is the fact that it has initiated a
new kind of entertainment for bazaars, garden fêtes, and
other summer diversions. The East has joined hands
with the West, and it has been found possible to have a
very passable series of gymkhana sports by using cycles

instead of ponies. That they are equal in interest is not to be expected. A pony, with its life and energy, is only feebly represented by the steel cycle. It may wobble and dance in a way distracting to its rider, if amusing to the looker-on, but the thousand and one "ways" of the smart polo pony heretofore used are missing.

However, in spite of this, a cycle gymkhana is no bad fare for an afternoon's amusement. It helps on a bazaar which might otherwise drag; it is a boon as an adjunct to a country flower show; and when all is said and done, it gives a large amount of skill in riding. Letter-posting against time off cycle back is not quite one of the easiest things imaginable. To dodge from one post to another, slipping in various-sized packages, checking the machine at exactly the right moment, using each hand impartially, knowing all the while that the seconds hand of the timekeeper's watch is flying round—all these do not conduce to make this particular gymkhana sport the child's play some would have us believe.

The site of operations should be a good big lawn or smooth field—the more room, the greater will be the success of the sports. If a course of 250 feet by 160 feet can be managed, so much the better for the tilting at the ring, V.C. race, etc.

The next thing is to recruit an efficient ground staff; men are indispensable, and military men are best. There must be a competent judge, whose word is law, and whose decisions must be clearly understood to be final. A notice to this effect should be placed at the foot of the ground rules, and hung up where every one can see it. Another indispensable official is the time-keeper, armed with a stop-watch. There must be two or three smart boys, under the orders of a volunteer clerk of the course, to hang up rings, replace the blocks when upset in the bending race, and make themselves generally useful. There must be a small tent set apart for cyclists' machines at twopence a machine, with a trustworthy man in charge. Each machine must have a label, and the owner receive a check, and no machine be given up without such check being returned. So much for the gymkhana staff. The posts for tilting at the ring may be made either of wood or iron. In the latter case it is best they should be made with a foot. The wooden ones require so large a hole that they are apt to injure the lawn, but the iron ones can be fitted without this drawback. The ring can be carried on a fixed hook, but it makes things a little less easy if a light wire is used, as at the Agricultural Hall tournaments. This sways in the wind, and requires more skill than if the ring is solidly fixed on a stout hook. The posts are put down each side of the ground, three a-side. The tilters run right hand inside, and the hooks or wires should be so arranged that the lance carries off the ring from the hook without resistance. If put on backwards a serious entanglement might result.

For the bending race, either large rubber balls or white wood blocks should be used. A white line should be run down the course, and a block placed upon it every six or seven feet. A cross mark of white should be made to indicate the exact place whereon to replace the block if knocked over. When there are two opposing teams, a couple of lines should be run parallel about twenty feet apart, and the marks and blocks be exactly alike. A white cross line should be run at one end, and a white painted post placed at the other, round which both competitors must go. To prevent mistakes, it is as well to station a man also.

The method of managing this race is to put each competitor level with the head of the line of blocks on the cross line. The starter inquires, "Are you ready?" the time-keeper takes the time, and at "Go" each one commences serpentining down her own line. It may be remembered, *en passant*, that it is a mistake to put on too great swing—it looks jerky. The first jerk means a still bigger one for the second block, and the fault once begun will end in a smash. On the other hand, starting straight *at* the line of blocks, and only swerving slightly, is the way to win. The pressure of the feet on the pedals should play an important part in the curves.

Letter-posting requires six letters. A bundle is handed to each competitor; generally it is two post-cards, two ordinary letters, and a couple of bulky ones, so large as to require a big shove to get them in the hole. These are the crucial ones, and are most likely to slip. If the rider drops one she must jump off, pick it up, mount, ride up again, and post off the machine. The letter-boxes are generally placed outside the tilting-posts. They can be made of straw-board, with the top to open so as to take out the letters—of course, also having the orthodox slit for posting. If painted red, they add much to the appearance of the ground.

The V.C. race can be elaborated either for men or ladies. In the former case hurdles and other obstacles add to the fun; in the latter it is required for one of each team to start level, pick up their dummy, and race back. A well-stuffed figure is rather awkward to handle, and quickness in stopping and dismounting has also to be studied.

Probably the most useful "gymkhana feat" is that of riding one machine and leading the other. It is simply a matter of knack. The rider gets the led machine close to her own, rather in the form of a "A." Using the led horse as a support, she springs up, catches the balance of both, and then rides off. The only thing is to mind that the led machine does not "straggle" away, and that, on the other hand, the pedals are well clear. Some guide by the end of the handles, others by the middle of the steering-bar. The latter gives most command.

Of course, the things which may be done on cycle-back are of an expansive kind. Probably a musical ride and tilting at the ring call for most skill. From inquiry I learn that Mr. W. Macpherson, of Sloane Street, can supply qualified assistants to go into the country and train teams at £1 per day, not including railway fare and accommodation. There can be no doubt about the beauty of a cycling musical ride, but all the riders would have to be faultless in the management of their machines.

The lances for tilting should be about four feet long. Billiard-cues can be used, but all should be of uniform length and thickness, and marked about half-way up for grasping aright. The rings should be burnished brass curtain-rings about the size of half-a-crown.

Bicycles for gymkhana work should be both low and close built. These are, of course, only suitable for park riding and fair weather riders, but the long wheel-base and larger wheels of a good roadster machine are not suitable to rapid mounts, dismounts, quick short turns, etc. For instance, in an egg and spoon race it is most difficult, if not quite impossible, to spring into the saddle without dropping the egg. The only way is to have a 26-inch wheeled machine, sit in the saddle, and push off with one leg. This is heretical to the last extent for good riding, but in fancy riding rules and regulations have sometimes to go to the wall. If obliged to use the ordinary roadster machine, it is best to put the saddle a trifle lower to facilitate rapid mounts and dismounts. A Swift is a close-built machine. So are some of the curve frame Rovers, also the "Modèle de Luxe."

In choosing a team, the organiser of the sports will do well to pick out the younger riders—even if they are not so practised as older ones. Activity scores highest in these sports. To be on and off like a flash, to be able to turn rapidly, are the things to aim at; in point of size, the smaller the rider the better. Older riders may do the tilting at the ring better, as it needs accuracy of eye and hand as well as strength and steadiness of pace, but as a rule, the younger the team the better.

Another feat, besides the outline ones mentioned, is—Vegetable race, each competitor having to fetch an assortment of onions, potatoes, cabbages, leeks, and carrots from a bucket at one end of the ground, and throw them into another without dismounting. This often produces comical results, as it is by no means easy to make an accurate shot from the saddle of a bicycle going fast. A scarf race is pretty, though somewhat of the nature of a cotillion figure. "Hands-off" races are dangerous when many are engaged.

9

Care of Machine

EVERY LADY who cycles should make a point of knowing how to repair her own machine when it goes wrong in minor ways, for there is nothing at all complicated in an up-to-date cycle. It is necessary to be able to locate a squeak, and apply remedial measures. A trifling irregularity in the chain may cause the machine to run heavily and make a horrible grinding noise. If the owner thoroughly understands her machine, and is able to do the minor repairs herself, it is very little more than the first cost she will require to pay, provided she uses average care in the handling of her cycle.

On the contrary, the one who always flies round to the repairer's shop for every click and squeak will find a pony come cheaper. If a machine is always having something done to it the expense mounts up ruinously.

That the bicycle should be kept clean and bright is only to be expected from every owner. It is the fashion to make a great parade about the cleaning, but ten minutes' steady work every day with a paraffin cloth and wash-leather suffices to keep both plate and enamel nice. It is when a machine is neglected—when the enamel gets dull and the plating tarnished—that a long time must be spent over it. One of the best adjuncts to a cleaner's outfit is a good stand, combined with a stand pump for inflating. By the use of this, the machine can be raised well off the ground, and the wheels and crank brackets cleaned with much greater ease than when the machine is on the ground.

In case of punctures to either wheel, it very much simplifies matters to take the entire wheel out of the frame and lay it on a bench or table. Then the outer cover—if a Dunlop—is worked off in the way clearly set forth in the book of instructions to be had from any depôt. Pulling the delicate inner tube out without taking off the cover entirely tends to bruise it, thus causing weak places and indirectly a tendency to burst. The front wheel is easy enough to manage. To repair the back one means that the gear-case must be removed. Take off the chain adjustment and slip off or unscrew the chain. It is not a nice job, but it is most useful to know how to do it. Once the wheel is off it is treated just the same as the front one.

For ladies' use, I can strongly recommend the Scottish tyre. There is absolutely no trouble entailed in removing the outer cover, and the tyre itself is of the first quality, and excellent in every way. I have had a pair fitted to my machine, and the result has been most satisfactory. The non-slipping tyre is very good, so much so, indeed, that I am rather inclined to prefer it even to the Dunlop-Welch.

The chain, whether protected by a gear-case or exposed to dust and mud in the miserable network frames which the rage for lightness has evoked, will require cleaning and attending to from time to time. If it runs in oil, in a Carter oil-bath case, it will require less than under other conditions; but if the gear-case be one of the leather variety, the dust and oil combined will cause a dirty chain which will need cleaning at intervals. The method of doing this is to take the chain right off, either by lifting off the cogs or taking out the screw which unites the links, and coiling it up in a tin pan full of paraffin. It should soak an hour or so—then be carefully rubbed dry and polished, so that no grit remains amongst the links. In replacing it, be sure that the worn side goes next to the cog-wheel. A chain put on wrong, if at all worn, can make a hideous noise, and quite destroy the owner's pleasure and comfort till it is set right. It is well to mark on a piece of paper the way the connecting link pointed before taking off. The head of the screw will be facing the owner, and the screw end the other side. Observation on these two points will prevent difficulty.

The ball-bearings, as a rule, are best left alone, but if it should be necessary to tighten or take them to pieces, great care must be taken not to screw them too tight. The best way is to screw them up tightly, then give the adjusting spanner a quarter turn back, which allows a certain amount of play. Then the locking-nuts must be screwed up carefully, and the wheels spun round. If they run freely, the weight of the pneumatic tyre valve should carry the wheel round at the last few revolutions. The Elswick and Centaur machines have disc-adjusting hubs. The buyer should obtain a thorough explanation of the right way to adjust these, as the plan differs from that mentioned here.

Sometimes a grating, grinding sound will come from the bearings, which denotes that a ball is broken. In this case, if unable to take the machine to a qualified man, the owner must lay the wheel or machine on its side and screw off the cover of the ball-bearings, taking the balls out one by one. As most machines are made on the interchangeable system, and duplicate balls can always be had by return post from the maker, this accident does not involve any serious trouble or expense. To get the balls back, they should be wiped clean from oil and rubbed in vaseline, a slight coating of which also should be run round the groove, to make them stick in their proper places whilst the cup cone is being screwed home. In the Elswick and Centaur machines the bearings are more complicated, being designed to resist dust, but with ordinary observation the replacing should be an easy task.

A broken spoke sometimes happens, generally after a railway journey; a few spare ones should, therefore, be kept at home with the lock-nuts into which the tangent spokes screw. To renew one of these, raise the tyre and inner tube, also the tape at the bottom of the rim which protects the air tube from rubbing on the spokes. Unscrew the old nut if the thread is worn out, take it out and replace by a new one. It requires care to get the spoke through the hole in the hub flange. It should be coaxed through, not bent or forced, and then held in a spoke grip whilst the nipple is turned, either by a special flat spanner or by the adjustable wrench. Care must be taken to get the spoke exactly the same tension as its fellows, or the rim will be pulled out of truth and have a tendency to buckle. The top of the new spoke will possibly require filing down flush with the head: a blacksmith can do this. If left it will injure the air tube. Buckled wheels require the help of an expert. They can be sprung back, but there is a certain knack in doing them, impossible to convey in writing.

A broken handle-bar, if of the fashionable twisted variety, is very difficult to manage. A straight bar can be easily made fit to use by the insertion of a piece of stick till a new one can be obtained. Those who are interested in the question of lightness should take out the handle-bar belonging to their machine, and they will be astounded at the ridiculously small weight of that imposing piece of plated metal.

The tools carried should receive more care than is generally the case. First should come a good wrench, and the owner should spend some time in learning how to use it. The way is to always apply the wrench sideways, screw it up squarely and firm, and then put on the pressure *steadily* and firmly. Little by little bring the whole force of the body to bear, and the nut must yield. To hurry and jerk is only to spoil both wrench and thread, and rasp the knuckles. Besides this wrench, a couple of plate-spanners, with holes to fit every nut on the machine, should be invested in for adjusting the saddle nuts, and those of the front and back wheel and handlebar. Spanners must be carried, and it is just as well they should fit exactly as badly. A spoke-grip is also useful. A small tyre-repairing outfit should be added; a length of rubber tubing, for renewing valves when they perish, as they will do in time; and an oil-can which will not leak, if such a thing can be obtained.

The best oil to use is that made by Tringham or Lucas. The best lubricant for the chain, if the gear-case is not an oil-bath, is Viscoleum or vaseline. Bearings in dusty weather should be washed out once a fortnight by squirting in paraffin. Oil up in wet weather more frequently than in dry; it prevents rust getting a hold of the bearings.

I often get laughed at for the ponderous contents of my tool-bag: "Such nonsense carrying about all that extra weight." Well, my critics might be right if the locality were blessed with a repairing-shop every mile or so—but if anything punctures or breaks, the nearest agent is eight miles off, and in my rides on the Wolds, if anything went wrong, it would be a case of either doing for oneself or carrying the machine. The other day my sister was riding along, when, wheeling their machines before a glorious rear wind, came two riders with punctured tyres. They inquired dolefully if there was any repairer, and the answer was, "Not within twelve miles." So they proceeded on their walking tour, no doubt wishing for the extra weight of a repairing outfit. In short, this craze for lightness is sheer folly; those who dispense with every needful thing go gaily for a while, but when accidents happen they are stranded. No one should stir out without a pump, repairing outfit, spanners, and oil-can. Accidents always happen just when they are particularly wanted not to—and if any one wishes to ascertain the value of their own pump, let them try to borrow one in the country, or extemporise a makeshift.

By knowing how to repair the machine, a ride becomes much more pleasant. It is the independence enjoyed that makes cycling so delightful, and this cannot be appreciated to the full without being quite self-contained. A village blacksmith is a most worthy man, as a rule, and can be trusted to carry out orders under supervision, but no one who values their cycle should leave it in untrained hands to mend while they take their ease elsewhere, or they will be sorry they did so.

General Hints

L IKE MOST OTHER SPORTS, cycling has its sunny
and cloudy sides. In moderation it is universally
conceded that the exercise is an excellent one for women
of all sorts and conditions. But in its very easiness and

delight lies the danger. Beginners will not be careful. They start off in companies for runs far too long, at a hurricane pace, and, once started, where is the one who will confess the pace too fast and drag behind? On they all will go—a regular case of "devil take the hindmost," and a few such mad runs will do untold mischief. Besides, this mode of proceeding is equally stupid and irrational. A man driving a good horse on a long journey will hold it in for the first few miles, and then gradually let it out to a good pace. Were he to begin by tearing off, as the cycling beginners do, he would have a beaten horse before half the journey was done. A good driver takes care of his cattle. A good rider will be careful to take much thought of herself. It is only the "feckless" bodies who start for a thirty miles ride at a good fourteen miles an hour pace, and then blame cycling if they break down. It does no harm to finish a run at a good swinging pace—the muscles have got into play, and used to the action—but to go the pace all through is more than any human being can stand.

It should be made a rule that the pace for the first few miles should not exceed eight miles an hour. Then the riders settle down, get their second wind, and can go on for twenty miles or more without rest or extra exertion. It is the same in mountaineering. Novices go off with a rush, meaning to polish off the mountain in no time:

"Lazy beggars," they say, "those guides, they never hurry themselves." Apparently this is true, but they are not lazy—and they *never stop*. The novice soon gives out, and is utterly exhausted at the end of a couple of hours, until she finds that "slow and sure wins the race," and is fain to, metaphorically, climb down and amend her ways.

Overdoing it on a cycle is really a dangerous and serious thing from every point of view; besides, the English cycle trade is responsible for a yearly increasing amount of prosperity, and it is highly important that the folly of foolish women should not give a splendid and health-giving sport a bad name. It does not deserve it. For fourteen years my sister and myself have ridden all sorts of machines, from the old single driving rear steerer, and when we did it in moderation we were all the better for it, and continue to be so. But it is very hard to be cautious; it is infinitely easier to sit and dogmatise, as I am doing now: the warning must, however, be given, and if my advice be taken in good part it will cause many happy rides to those who read this weary preachment. If once a rider overdoes herself, it means months, even years of care to get right again.

Probably nothing is a greater help to taking things easily than cultivating a pet hobby, such as, for instance, sketching. There are so many pretty quaint bits get-at-able on the cycle, simply making one long to transfer them to the sketch-book, which is an agreeable reminder of past rides, as well as of absorbing present interest. The requisites either for oil or water colour are so easily carried, and the cycle is such a help, it is a wonder that more cycling sketching-clubs are not formed. Painting has a great advantage over photography in the fact of the reproduction of colours. A dry plate can present a scene in faultless detail, but it is the colour, the atmosphere, the gold of the corn on the ruddy earth against the blue of the sky, and the wonderful purple shadows, which convey much meaning. The sketcher can reproduce these, but we photographers can only strive after distance and fuzzy effects, which some call artistic but others "blurred." Every cyclist who can sketch should sketch. Either tripod or easel can be carried in a pair of metal handle-bar carriers, costing 1*s*. 3*d*.

If not, it is a good thing to carry a small film hand-camera. The cycle photographer is ubiquitous, and if his work is not artistic, it forms a pleasant reminiscence of a tour. With photography may be bracketed archaeology. This is a most fascinating pursuit—very far from being the dry-as-dust affair some think. Then with this, works in heraldry, the forming a collection of old sun-dials, or extraordinary epitaphs on monuments. I have come across some very quaint ones in country churchyards. Natural history is a fit hobby for cycling. Mounted on rubber-tyred wheels, the manners and customs of birds, beasts, and even reptiles may be studied—for it is possible to get quite close to them without being heard. Anything is better than a long, solitary ride along a straight road. If possessed of no hobby or companion, carry a book, and read over dull stretches of flat country. But, really, most riders, except the scorching fraternity, learn to find such interest in the newness of everything—people, cottages, the country and all, that the very change itself is an interest.

To descend off the hobby-horse to the mundane side of life, cyclists, like horses, should be good feeders. They should start work with coffee and toast, and either an egg or two or ham—with both, if the latter is not too rich. Half-an-hour after this, but not later than nine o'clock A.M., they should be *en route* until twelve. In the sultry days of July and August the wise rider will carry a good lunch—sandwiches, biscuits, claret, chocolate, raisins, and other oddments—and have a quiet picnic in the shade, with either a companion to chat to, or a favourite author to renew acquaintance with.

It is best to rest during the heat of the day, from twelve to three, and proceed in the cool of the afternoon, reaching the destination about five or six P.M. A bath, change, and good plain dinner should follow, then either a stroll or a pleasant chat, and bed. The rider should sleep like a top, and be up by seven the next morning, fresh and bright. Coffee, if it can be got good, is best to start on. Abroad one can generally depend on the coffee, if on nothing else, but in England it is so difficult to get good, that Schweitzer's cocoatina is the best alternative. Tea in the morning disagrees with many people. Porridge, for those who like it, is superb training fare. Drink on the way should be milk and soda—not pure milk, which, on a hot day, is apt to produce bad effects.

Riding in the full glare of the sun should be avoided. The vital part to protect against sunstroke is the back of the neck, just above the collar. If the sun beats fiercely on this part, the coat collar should be turned up, or a thick silk muffler worn. We English expose ourselves to the sun; Arabs and Indians wrap up their heads to ward off the rays, and they are decidedly the wiser.

Many ladies' clubs are now being started, and, from some points of view, those who are alone in their rides might do worse than join them. But women are not, as a rule, fitted for club life. They are not so broad-minded as men—they have an infinity of social rings, one within the other, and when in authority are apt to be arbitrary and tyrannical. Probably the best exclusively ladies' club is the Lady Cyclist Association, which has branches (rather imitating the organisation of the Cyclists' Touring Club) in most of the large towns. One of the oldest cycling clubs for ladies is the Coventry Ladies'—Miss Edith Thomas, captain. Another has recently been started in Newcastle-on-Tyne, and district associations of the Cyclists' Touring Club are either formed, or being formed, all over England.

Riding in company is a certain safeguard against annoyance from tramps, though I think a lady, inconspicuously dressed and riding quietly alone in daylight, has little to fear. However, in the vicinity of large manufacturing towns the rowdy element may at times annoy ladies riding alone, though I have, myself, always met with the greatest kindness and courtesy; still, this may have been by exceptional good fortune, and I have no wish to boast of it.